THE POWER OF REALISTIC THINKING IN TODAY'S WORLD

Matt Roberts-Ward
Sharon Mitchell

Copyright © 2023 Matt Roberts-Ward
Copyright © 2023 Sharon Mitchell

The moral right of the author has been asserted.

Apart from any fair dealing for the purposes of research or private study, or criticism or review, as permitted under the Copyright, Designs and Patents Act 1988, this publication may only be reproduced, stored or transmitted, in any form or by any means, with the prior permission in writing of the publishers, or in the case of reprographic reproduction in accordance with the terms of licences issued by the Copyright Licensing Agency. Enquiries concerning reproduction outside those terms should be sent to the publishers.

Matador
Unit E2 Airfield Business Park,
Harrison Road, Market Harborough,
Leicestershire. LE16 7UL
Tel: 0116 2792299
Email: books@troubador.co.uk
Web: www.troubador.co.uk/matador
Twitter: @matadorbooks

ISBN 978 1803136 820

British Library Cataloguing in Publication Data.
A catalogue record for this book is available from the British Library.

Printed and bound in Great Britain by 4edge Limited
Typeset in 11pt Minion Pro by Troubador Publishing Ltd, Leicester, UK

Matador is an imprint of Troubador Publishing Ltd

1

THE GOOD, THE BAD AND THE UGLY CONVERSATIONS WITH MYSELF

SHARON

How important is authenticity to you?

What is the difference between what others see and who we actually are?

Is faking it to make it just making us lonelier?
Sometimes I meet people who seem, for at least some of the time, to be what I term their 'Facebook selves'. Perfect clothes, perfect looks, perfect meals (every time), perfect holidays, perfect family, perfect relationship.

I recall one of my service users saying, 'Anyone who smiles that much must have something wrong with them.'

I remember my younger self smiling, too.

Smiling to head off emotional abuse.

Smiling when the abuse was underway.

Keeping smiling after the abuse… if there is discord in my relationship, isn't it my job to mitigate it, or if I can't, mop up afterwards with minimum fuss?

It's my job to look after my family, too, even when their abuse would never be tolerated by anyone outside the family circle.

It's all part of being a good daughter, sister, partner, friend. It's what women do!

I'm smiling wryly as I write this, because my authentic self, as I see it, is a socialist and feminist. Fighting for equality. Fighting for justice. Fighting for freedom. Challenging discrimination.

Someone who makes sure not to bring any injustice or inequality to my yard.

Yet here they are, sapping my life, making sure I don't do right by myself.

My body knows this; every time I have a headache (which was pretty much all the time), every time my IBS flares up, every time it has to process yet another party or night out, every time I overeat, which again was pretty much all the time.

My mind lies and lies again, telling me I'm free and powerful, and that this is the price.

My real self was something to be ashamed of, something I had to hide away. I got the message from my parents, unwittingly or not, that I was disgusting. I remember my childhood as one punctuated by criticism, and often felt belittled. I remember enraged arguments that seemed to be there for the sake of arguing. I was accused of 'always having to have the last word'. Usually, I was so scared of the consequence if I dared to show my authentic self, it felt safer not to have any words – to not speak at all. Sometimes I could no longer stay quiet and would explode into molten rage, screaming the most hurtful things I could think of. Result: being blamed for being 'dramatic' and 'blowing things out of all proportion'. End result: more shame, more self-disgust.

None of us can control what others think of us, but as a child, what the adults approve or don't approve of in us is a matter of survival. There may be a consequence for us that is frightening, if we dare to show our real selves. I became a terrible liar in self-defence; telling the truth might be catastrophic. In adulthood, I have been lucky to meet people who affirm me and help me to build my self-esteem, although this has taken a long time. I enjoy the life I have made and strive to feel at optimum level in regard to my health, my relationships, my finances and my future. I continue with the work of loving myself and try to believe that I am enough.

Learning (and now teaching) mindfulness has been so important in helping me into my authentic life. Self-awareness, moment to moment, is my safe haven and unbreakable foundation. Covering over my own needs had become second nature, but mindfulness teaches us to recognise what it is we need, and to lovingly do right by ourselves, and to be a light for others. I'm thankful that I am not now aggressive or judgemental in my conversation, and so can more easily connect with people and keep my self-esteem.

I'm conscious of the need to keep my worst self out of my mouth, but also need to check in with myself during a social interaction to make sure that I'm not editing something that needs to be said or needs to be felt. I sometimes speak in shorthand, so that the message is unclear (and therefore not questioned), or leave out details, for the same reason. Remember, saying how I feel was, at best, inconvenient and, at worst, shameful, and my feeling is that it still might be.

I couldn't control what others thought of me as a child and, paradoxically and joyfully, I still can't. It is not my business. Mindfulness has taught me to let go of attachment to the outcomes of interactions and relationships (in the Buddhist tradition, attachment is one of the roots of all suffering). My business is to grow my secure self and trust that I can bring the right people into my life, and that I deserve to have them there.

To conclude, I'm continuing the long walk towards my best self, with others who are doing the same. The negative people, the users and the abusive, are much more quickly identified and burn themselves out due to lack of my attention or are themselves burnt away. In the heat of the fire, I am making a new world, more generous and truer than ever before, and the price of my freedom cannot be my own silence. My authentic self depends on it.

2

ABOUT ME

MATT

I am writing this book about the power of positive thinking because it has been a lifelong ambition of mine. To share with people through examples of my own so that they can recognise how to change their lives for the better.

I have been very fortunate in the way my life has enabled me to grab hold of opportunities and learn about what is important. To begin with, I learned in my early years to use my imagination and to be very comfortable with my own company – I would often spend time on the climbing frame in the back garden just watching my dad doing gardening and looking after the plants and flowers. Then I learned how to be creative and cook simple recipes by mixing together different ingredients. After this, sadly, my dad died and I went into what I now know is an in-between place where you are stuck working and being safe without really seeing outside of that. Oddly, at the time, I worked at a coffee shop called 'Reflections' and one friend, at the time, commented how I was unable to see my own reflection or my way. I had the perception that my worth was a person who could only wipe tables. What could possibly be wrong with it? The customers loved me. I was always smiling and yet I was sad inside.

Eventually, a friend gave me Louise Hay's *You Can Heal Your Life* and Susan Jeffers' *Feel the Fear and Do it Anyway*. I can thoroughly recommend both of these books as shortly after reading these, I left my job. Then I woke up and went to do an access course in Social Care and before I knew it was choosing universities. Blimey, life sure moves fast when your eyes are open and paying attention! I chose nine universities and ended up getting accepted at two: one in Cambridge at a college and the other in Preston, Lancashire. I turned down Cambridge and moved to Preston. I lived a life of partying for a year as if I was a teen (after missing out on being a teen when my dad died at twelve): going out most nights to the local student bar, and belonging to the mountaineering group, the badminton group and the cinema club. It was one year-long party.

Then, reality hit as I realised that it was time to heal. I decided to have Cruise counselling and deal with the death of my dad and get some closure. Then, to go on a five-month study exchange in Portugal. After three months, I was feeling a lot better as I wanted to be away and learn who I was again. I did and found I liked cooking, history, my own space and languages, and I loved being in Portugal. I got to know the local school community and helped with Portuguese children learning English. I travelled round Portugal and saw the Algarve, and went to Madrid and took in the sights and food. Then it was time to come home and back to university with one big decision: was I quitting after two years or was I staying?

To everyone in my course, it seemed like madness. I only had a year to go and yet I was leaving to do art. Everyone was like 'Are you crazy?', but I knew it was right. I had discovered that I liked art while in Portugal and wanted to explore it further. I knew in my heart it was a huge gamble but the thought of not doing something I wanted for a year was too much and I left university for a Foundation Art course in Manchester – and have not looked back. I discovered in that year that I could draw and, indeed, create paintings. I ended the year with paintings that delighted everyone – my shadow paintings. These were paintings of shadows from sandwich boards to shadows on the pavement or fences and they were amazing.

In one year, I had changed my life for good. I had opened up the left side of my brain and now saw everything totally differently. The power of taking a risk can be huge when you try. Then I went to university again in Salford to do a Visual Arts course and I got a second. Not bad, eh, for a person who came out of school with only three GCSES and a belief that all he was capable of was going to catering college. My end degree show was of fabric sculpture and seeing the shapes that are left behind by a broken wine bottle. All the time, seeing the unseen and allowing it to become real. So, even back then, I knew I wanted to bring awareness to how there is always something else that is not seen.

This, again, was not where I stopped and instead of going into art I went into a relationship and moved to Worthing. There, I did a hypnotherapy course and learned about the power of being able to create change in people's lives through their intuition. I was able to give people more confidence, enable them to overcome their fear of lifts, break free from the thoughts that were preventing them from moving forwards and to heal some long-held fears associated with their childhood. Still, I was not content and knew this was not the end of my journey. Now, I was moving into a period of change and development of me as a person. To work with people, I had to learn about people.

So, I joined networking groups and mixed with other entrepreneurs. I got involved in going to the meeting and running a networking group for two years in Shoreham called 'A Great Get Together'. This was very successful and regularly had ten participants who came and shared and felt as though they not only had fun, but also gained from being there as they learned about themselves. This showed me that I was able to work with people and gave me a confidence that I had been lacking prior to this. Following on from this, I became a support worker with learning difficulties and learned about how to see life from their perspective. How to communicate in different ways and the importance of understanding their needs and supporting them.

This, again, opened my eyes to seeing the needs of the

individual and them being able to have the right to make choices that are not influenced by me in any way. I did this for seven years before I decided it was time to learn more and I changed jobs to be a teaching assistant and work with children. This is where I am now and is by far the most fulfilling work as well as the most challenging. I know my journey has still further to go and this is why me and Sharon are writing this book as it is time to give back to you, the reader, our experiences and show you how you can change your life through making different choices. I am a trained hypnotherapist and counsellor. I can cook anything and have the patience to both listen and support anyone to see their lives differently through my work with learning disabilities and children.

3

MISSING THE BOAT

MATT

I don't know about you, but don't you just hate it when things go wrong? Everything is planned and you know when you have to be somewhere and what time it is and still somehow life goes against you. Well, this happened to me and Sharon when we were due to get a boat from Portsmouth to the Isle of Wight.

We both set off at the correct time and met at Worthing Station. Then we got on the train going to Portsmouth, or so we thought, until we realised it was actually going to Southampton. Aah! Did we panic? No, we just thought we could get off in a minute and catch the right train. This was totally different to how the male character reacted in *Clockwise* where he got on the wrong train when he misunderstood the guard, who, when asked if it was the correct train, said 'Right'. Then the man asking got off the correct train and got on the wrong one. Seconds later, he heard where the train he was on was going whilst seeing his train leaving the station. He had no time to catch it and panic ensued. Thankfully, we got off our train and crossed over the platform to catch a train going back to Portsmouth and were able to see the situation calmly.

Now we were back enroute to Portsmouth and the weather had unfortunately taken a turn for the worse and it was raining. Despite this, we were determined to make our boat crossing at Portsmouth. We arrived in Portsmouth with minutes to spare and saw our boat leaving. We literally could have lost the plot and swore or thought, *Why us?*. Instead, we chose to have a rethink and consider the possibility that maybe this could benefit us. I know it's crazy but it's true. We decided to delay going to the Isle of Wight till the afternoon and to get some lunch. The rain was now really heavy and looked as though it was here to stay.

We decided to make the best of what seemed like a horrible situation and find some lunch in Portsmouth. We put up our umbrellas and made our way towards the shopping area known as Gunwharf Quays. There, we tried a few restaurants until we found one that would be opening at noon. We nearly jumped for joy, as our prayers had been answered – we had a shelter from the rain and somewhere to eat.

We enjoyed the dryness of the seats outside the restaurant under cover until it opened and felt grateful for missing the boat and giving us this opportunity. Then, when the restaurant opened, we could not have been more pleased as they served vegan burgers, mayo and ketchup. This, to me and Sharon, was as though all our dreams had come true. We both love vegan food and a lot of the time have vegan food without mayo or ketchup, and the options are not nearly as good. Here, not only were there vegan burgers, but also other options. Also, they served ginger beer and we both love ginger beer. On top of this was the offer of eating out to help out and so we got one meal for half price. We literally could not get over how missing that boat had opened up this experience to us and we both could not have been happier.

4

PERFECT STRANGER

SHARON

Matt and I like nothing better than a relaxed tasty meal during our travels (which we aim to walk off, but because we are a work in progress, not perfect, this doesn't always happen). But we remember this mealtime in particular.

Eating for us is both comfort and joy, a counterpoint to troubling times, and a way to give and receive love, to surprise and inspire. It is rarely one more task in a day, although occasionally that will happen. New eating houses give us reason for happiness, and another reason to enjoy life, even if it's about not wanting to cook or wash up. Lockdown has meant that we appreciate this so much more (the attitude of gratitude) and it has given us an opportunity to practise turning ruminative thoughts upside down – we miss the chance to go out and explore, but we also hold hope for the future. Lockdown will change, and then end, as most things do.

We didn't really have any major expectations of our day. We were in lockdown for the first time, so we knew that not much would be open. We decided to sit with this situation and enjoy what would come. We didn't expect perfection; we were going to be realistic. We didn't fall into the trap of asking each other (or somebody else) for reassurance about what might happen. We knew that we could handle whatever would happen; we have worked hard on developing our emotional confidence and handling difficult emotions and decisions.

As I write, it is springtime, and the daffodils, one of my favourite flowers, are in full bloom. In amongst the beautiful yellow blooms, I have occasionally been surprised to find daffodils of other colours – ones that are almost all white, with just a hint of pale lemon in the centre, and one that has pink inner petals and a white exterior. They remind me of our visit to the island on this day and how we found the perfect stranger – the wise man in the ordinary.

We were looking for a place to have lunch, but there were few places to choose from, and not many places that looked inviting. We settled on an ordinary-looking café with fairly ordinary choices as to what to eat. A customer asked us if we were strangers to the island. I was getting the impression that this was a place where not much happened, and one that probably didn't embrace difference in many ways. I thought, *Probably best to do what we need to do, then leave as soon as possible. Nothing to see here.*

I felt myself tuning in to the conversation of the man behind the counter. He was serving someone with a roast dinner and talking about, of all things, Buddhism.

Turns out the man was a practising Buddhist who, of course, knew a lot about mindfulness and meditation. He had lived in London for a long time. I had completely misread him, assuming from his business and his workwear that he would not have an interest. In the middle of the most commonplace of circumstances, he was staying true to, and happily sharing, his personal values. He was the flower in the bunch who was equally beautiful but different. We felt blessed to be in his company and slightly ashamed to have jumped to conclusions about who this person was. We had not taken the time to see that the picture didn't fit our expectations or assumptions. Yet he had not judged us and was happy to share his wisdom with us. His vision of himself and of us was non-judgemental and accepting, not clouded by his anxieties. The sting of our embarrassment reiterated the lesson; our way is not the only way of understanding a person or situation, particularly if our viewpoint isn't underpinned by much factual evidence and relies on opinion instead.

As we left the café, we weren't sure of the right path to where we needed to go, or even where that was!

We found the bus station and got on a bus to anywhere, trusting in ourselves to manage the journey and whatever it brought. We found a beautiful old village to enjoy, had the obligatory coffee and an ice cream, and resolved to return one day to finish exploring. We made the return journey in the warmth and colour of a summer evening.

We got off at a stop we hadn't expected, so got a little lost on the way back to the railway station. We weren't worried about this, allowing our anxieties to cloud our peace and our judgement. What was the worst that could happen? If we got lost, it wouldn't be a disaster; it would be something we would be adequate for, as we had been many times before. Our experience is an opportunity, not tainted by someone else's conditions or expectations.

I put opinion, and my fears, before the facts. I get some situations out of proportion. I think of the worst thing that could happen; but in this small café, the best thing presented itself. My friend has a saying; 'It is what it is'. My personal vision now is to acknowledge the rubies in the dust, the hidden jewels in the everyday, with a peaceful curiosity. It's only my fear that needs to change. The world doesn't need to be better, or different, on my account. It is taking its course, purely and simply.

It is what it is.

5

WHAT'S ON THE MENU?

MATT

I don't know about you, but I am a person who likes to be organised. I like to know what I am going to be eating and what ingredients I am going to need to make it. You could say I am a born organiser and seldom leave things to chance. So much so that my wife now tells me when she is leaving something out, so I don't tidy it away. Anyway, today was different. My colleague, Sharon, was treating me to a meal out for my birthday. I didn't know where we were going and what we were going to be having. I literally was putting my trust in her hands. Was I worried? Not in the least, as I knew everything would turn out as it was supposed to.

I met Sharon after she had finished at a collection for the homeless. She had been at the hall where it was taking place all morning and people had been bringing in donations. The words generous don't begin to describe what people had given. I was blown away at how people had not just emptied their cupboards. They had gone a whole lot further than that and gone out and bought brand-new bedding and crockery sets. It was great to see and truly inspiring. I met Sharon and helped her to load the rest of the donations into the volunteer driver's van. He was volunteering his time to transport the donations from this hall to a venue where they could be given to the homeless people who desperately needed them. Sharon locked up and we left for our next adventure.

To begin with, we weren't sure where we were going to go and discussed a few options before deciding to get the train to Hove. I remembered a Moroccan restaurant that we had both enjoyed before. Enroute, we chatted about how fortunate we both felt to have been able to experience the beauty of nature recently on our travels. How it was lovely to see the flowers and to see nature in all its magnificence. We talked about how we were enjoying the opportunity of coming out of lockdown. The chance to really see nature again and appreciate how we both felt gratitude at experiencing what had always been there but, somehow, we had not seen before. Sounds strange, I know, but it was like we were really seeing everything around us again: the butterflies, flowers, the colours and different shades of buildings that were suddenly truly special.

Along our journey to the train station, we passed by the corner House pub, and me and Sharon both said how nice the food was in there. Then we got our tickets at the train station to go to Hove. As was customary when travelling on the train, we both put on our face masks and found some seats. The train was not very busy and we were soon in Hove. The journey seemed to take very little time and then we were on our way to the Moroccan restaurant. On the way we talked about our theatre trip that was coming up to see Frida Kahlo. This had been postponed because of lockdown and was now due to be in a weeks' time. We arranged to meet before the performance at a vegan restaurant. After a while we were near the restaurant, and I was excited to go and experience their food again. We hadn't booked and were taking it that business would be quiet after the scheme 'Eat Out to Help Out' had ended and restaurants were now not so busy.

We entered the restaurant and put on our face masks, as this was now mandatory. Upon entering we found the restaurant to be empty and were really pleased, as we would have time to chat whilst enjoying good food. We asked for a menu after being greeted and shown to a table. We both decided to have some hot and cold starters, and these consisted of houmous and pitta bread, aubergines, feta cheese in pastry and vine leaves. Alongside this they brought us some hot pitta bread and our drinks. It was great; the food was in front of us and we both felt truly grateful for such tasty food. The restaurant was also very beautiful with a wooden sculpture of fishes in a net on the wall and an open-plan kitchen so we could see the chef at work.

We enjoyed our starters whilst talking about all our adventures so far. From missing a boat and avoiding bad weather to getting a train back when, from the outset, there seemed to be no trains going to where we wanted to go – and yet, instead of panicking, we got back. Also, how we had witnessed the beauty of one disused canal and another one that was seen as a cycle path and walkway rather than a thing of beauty. Also, how we had delighted in a ruined cathedral and an old castle, which both told many stories. All in all, in a really short space of time, we had managed to experience lots of amazing and wonderful adventures. Least of all was walking along the South Downs and discovering an old water wheel and a tunnel of trees, which was truly breath-taking and mesmerising.

Then, as if given to me, I realised these adventures were a gift and we needed to share them with everyone in a book. I told Sharon and she agreed, and this is what has now led to this being one of the chapters of this amazing book you are now reading. Yes, you, the reader, are travelling with us and experiencing our ups and downs like we both experienced them. What an amazing gift to be able to share with you all the places, sights and things we had done. To say I was ecstatic really does not do this moment justice. I was buzzing with ideas and how much this was the beginning of something truly special for me and Sharon.

Anyway, back to the meal, which was truly satisfying. We had finished the starters and were ready for the main course, which we had decided to share, and it did not disappoint. The tastes and flavours were amazing. It was like having a bag of sweets and every mouthful had a different taste from spices to herbs and aubergines. Then there were the tomatoes and onions and other vegetables.

It was amazing. I felt spoilt by my friend, Sharon. We finished with a coffee as we both love our coffees and then Sharon insisted on paying and I said, 'Thank you' and that she was too kind. Then we enjoyed the chocolates and left after saying 'Thank you' to the staff. It was truly a great meal; we had had exactly what we desired and were well and truly fed.

There is an understanding that you may or may not know and it is about manifestation. You can bring about exactly what you need when you put yourself in the right place. To explain this simply: when you have no plans and open yourself up to possibilities in life, you can give yourself exactly what you need. This takes a certain amount of risk and only happens when you fully put yourself in a place of openness and vulnerability to accept that things may or may not work out. Then you can truly be in a place where you can allow things to come to you, such as great food, a friend getting in contact with something you have been looking for, or a book or item of clothing you have had your eye on and suddenly it is yours. This is truly magical and is more than possible when you truly break free from having to have a plan and be organised. So even though I am organised, I am also someone who can just as easily let go and let the wonders of life in.

I leave you with our last discovery and again this was unplanned. We got to the train station and immediately I went to cross over to the other platform as the trains home were going from that platform. We got over there and the train we needed was on the other platform where we had come from. Strange, I know, but why would life be playing tricks on me and Sharon? The answer I realised was simple. It was another lesson from life and this was 'Don't expect things to be the way you think they are, and expect the unexpected'. Wow, crazy, I know, and yet so mind-blowing. In life, don't think things are going to be the way they were as things change and you need to not always try so hard. In other words, life is fluid and changeable. No amount of preparation is going to prepare you for something simple, as often by planning it can be overlooked and missed. So, enjoy life's little accidents.

6

DIFFERENT LIGHT

SHARON

Humans have a strong instinct to touch each other in greeting. Handshakes, kisses and hugging are common to many cultures, and help to build trust and bond people together (Black, R M, 2011). Proximity to another person's bodily aroma enables us to assess their physical and emotional state.

During lockdown, extended social contact has been prohibited, to lessen the threat of spreading disease, yet we still wish to have social contact with family and friends, and that may include hugging and kissing them. We want to signal that our bond of love and friendship is still strong. Even though our social circle can still transmit coronavirus, we find the instinct for physical contact very difficult to avoid.

At the time of writing the above, my friend A was still alive, although we both knew they had only months, if not weeks, to live. They died this month, amidst the first sunshine of the spring.

Because of the Coronavirus pandemic, we had not met in person for over a year, although we had kept in touch on the phone, and we exchanged birthday cards and gifts through the post.

I loved my friend very much, and we had a very deep connection in many ways, whilst feeling free to disagree on some things. I told her several times I loved her before she died, although I feel blessed to know that she was always aware of this, and we both know that her death won't change it.

So shouldn't that be enough?

I'm not being callous or glib in this. The death of a loved one is shocking and painful, and our unhappiness is part of the price of losing them. But for whom do we grieve?

I can't do anything more in this life for my friend. So who is my sadness for?

It's partly for family and friends who have also lost them, but I have to acknowledge and accept, however difficult that some of it is also for myself.

And that makes me feel selfish, guilty and hateful.

I started to search the internet to see if anyone else had dared to be so unkind. What I found was surprising.

Buddhists writing about grief would say that the feeling of grief is due to an attachment to the person that has been unfairly destroyed. It implies that the person was seen as a belonging, there to be enjoyed in real time. We struggle to accept the reality of our loss. We argue for the restoration of our 'rights'. We demand our own way. We want our love back. None of this is realistic, helpful or mindful, since it is not about the acknowledgement and acceptance of the situation – a key element of mindfulness.

I want A to still be alive, for me, with our world, and our identity. I don't want to die myself.

I am selfish because this is for me, not her.

I want what could be. I'm not living in the here and now, not being mindful, and certainly not being realistic.

My attachment to the way things should be is putting me at war with myself and deepening my grief.

A knew that everything in life changes and ends, including life itself. They wanted me to accept this and told me so during our last conversation. A knew they were dying, and fully acknowledged and accepted this.

My work now is to try to do the same.

In mindfulness, we learn that everything is impermanent. Pain and fear come and goes, with shifting degrees of intensity. Some of my pain has already happened; some of my tears are to come. There will be changes over time and I will probably go through different stages of the grieving process (Kubler Ross, 1969): denial, anger, bargaining, sadness and, finally, the peace of acceptance.

I know I will want to scream and make a scene, argue with God, and wish for just one more day with her for a good while yet. I would do anything to be able to hug my friend one last time. The tyranny of the 'should be' is mine to hold, but my thoughts are mine to change. In refusing to let go, I attach myself to a past that has already dissolved and use my mind to destroy my future. Their memory is not against me, A's light is for me. My time is now.

MEANINGFUL POETRY PIECES

DUALITY

The moonlight shimmered to the dark of the night
Blackness surrounding everywhere except
the luminescent shadow on the lake.
As if trapped in the sequential segments of time
The light refused to surrender to the darkness
threatening its very being.
Bats and owls swirled revelling in this window of light.
Delighting in the gift given to them by mother nature
Insects whirled and whizzed around angrily at being
woken from their night slumber.
Buzzing this way and that, shooting backwards and
　　forwards
from lily pads to leaves.
Engrossed in their anger and despair at the moon being
　　so bright.
The iciness of the lake from the cold would not fully
　　freeze.
Feeling a sense of happiness, the lake indulged in this
　　brightness.

The night sky was displeased and determined to dispel this light.
It called upon the rain to disperse dark clouds full of fiery rain.
Darting down heavily on the peace of the lake the shots dispelled
the light core fragmenting it away leaving only darkness in its wake.

INSPIRATION

Ideas buzzing around like bees in a hive.
Leaping forwards off a diving board.
Pen racing across the page with excitement.
Energy bursting forth into action.
Crescendo of music as fireworks blast into the sky.
Thoughts turn into reality.
Springing into action and taking form.
Creating beautiful expressions of active dynamics.

THE SUREST GUIDE

Life doesn't give us much sometimes.
So, when it does, take heed and notice.
These can be the smallest things
such as a new badge or picture which is overdue.
The other guides can be a friend suddenly
offering an opportunity for change.
These are life or intuition allowing you to see

that it's time for a change.
The smallest things that come to you when you
least expect it like a song that won't go away.
That niggling feeling that you need to be somewhere
or call someone up these are again guides to take.
Overlooking these guides will not harm you straightaway
but can over time cause you anxiety or stress.
The guides in their own way were there to stop you
from dealing with changes or disharmony which was coming.
Life doesn't offer throw us many curveballs but when it does
take heed and follow them no matter how bizarre.
When a door opens it opens for a reason and this is
sometimes scary and yet also can be transformative.
So, take the leap and defy the odds you can change anytime.

CHOICES

Is a choice ever wrong?
Depends on the options.
How confident the outcome?
Whether any learning
Can take place.
Choices are different each time.
One choice can be the worst.
Open a door to something better.
While another choice can be
right and yet wrong as it
takes you away from yourself.
Choices are gifts to receive.

PERSPECTIVE

Seeing is believing they say.
Viewpoints are different.
Depending on where you are.
Up a mountain
or in a valley.
To say the glass is half full
speaks volumes when emotional.
Discarded view not visible
Too many thoughts cause distraction.
Similarly, when making decisions
Viewpoint is less clear
when dominated with indecision.
The obvious can be overlooked.
Never easy to see everything.
Until focus is clearer
With silence and clarity.
A true picture stands tall.
Within reach and aligned.

AWKWARDNESS

Smells like smelly feet from mucking around at the farm.
Tastes like aromatic juicy oranges mixed with hot
    peppercorn.
Sounds like the engine of a car revving when it's trying to
    start.
Feels like wet sea splashing me, while standing against
    sharp rocks.

Looks like a sunny day with rain splashing down from invisible clouds.
Awkwardness is the element of life which keeps us on our toes.

7

FOOD FOR THOUGHT

SHARON

It used to be the case that mental health professionals/nurses were not usually well known for a healthy lifestyle and a personal focus on wellbeing. Unsocial hours, the stress of the job and a habit of raising our energies via a variety of sugary and fatty foods didn't do us any favours in terms of health. Our habits (coffee with four sugars anyone?) didn't serve us, either physically or mentally. Our bad habits became entrenched over time, and since most of us seemed to have them, we rarely questioned them, or we let our negative thoughts about changing cloud our judgement (I really need a drink/cigarette after that shift from hell/I'm not going to start cooking at 10pm/Drink water? With what?)

My body wasn't going to support me in my fifties, sixties and beyond by staying the same. One benefit of changing would be the avoidance of chronic sickness and/or an early death. A lot of my mother's family died from heart disease and many of them were paid-up members of the Yorkshire pudding club. In terms of my mental health, cigarettes, alcohol and cholesterol-filled snacks won't lift moods beyond the short term (in fact, long-term use of alcohol actually contributes to depression and anxiety in many users).

Both very meaningful reasons to change, but, as with any ingrained long-term habit, it looked like a lot of effort for not many biscuits.

And a change would take away something that was my ally as well as my enemy. Something dependable and destructive at the same time.

I have found out that binge eating can be a way to self-medicate if you're suffering from anxiety or depression, and that it can be a diversion away from thoughts stemming from trauma. Binge drinking (or what, during our nurse training, was just called drinking) is also seen as being something that can be used to feel less anxious. Plus a group drink in the evening was a social norm, again, a habit, and one that was almost expected. If I had one spare evening as a student nurse, it was one too many, and most of my friends and workmates felt the same way. Smoking was much more acceptable at the time and many nurses smoked with gusto. Why not, after 10 days straight at work? It was that or (another) sick day. Most of us believed strongly that these interventions were essential for relaxation.

Additionally, the guilt and shame attached to negative thoughts about overeating could sometimes lead to feelings of anger, which in turn led to more eating (I'm at work all the time! I'm exhausted! Why can't I have something nice? Everybody else does!)

I was a smoker for around twenty-five years, and for most of that time I had very mixed feelings about giving up. Smoking was a great pleasure, and the act of smoking seemed to help me to destress (probably because I was inadvertently breathing mindfully). I wasn't very confident in my ability to stop and tried many times without success. Each time I started again, the negative thoughts would crowd in, and I felt hopeless and disgusting. This led, in turn, to heavier smoking.

I learnt through my mindfulness training and practice that we are not our thoughts. We are observers of our thoughts and they are in our control. Resistive thoughts only have the power that we give them. If we wish to change, we must try to let our resistive thoughts go and move into our futures.

One thought that helped me to change was this: 'I am choosing to change, because I want to'. Another was: 'I know what I need to change, because I have insight. I'm going to find the best way to make a change'.

This meant that I was the instigator of the change, the one in control, the one with the power. This felt good.

So, when those negative thoughts hit me hard, I hit them right back. I built up an armoury of realistic/positive thoughts, with the evidence to back them up. I worked hard, and gave myself praise and credit for working hard.

I became aware of some of my common triggers for

overeating, binge smoking and drinking, which turned out to be the usual suspects. Anxiety, mild depression, insomnia, boredom. Having not looked too much at my triggers (because I thought I couldn't change), they were on permanent automatic repeat. Once I had brought them into the light, I could then make a change. For instance, if I'm not occupied, I might fill that time with food. If I can't sleep, a doughnut or two is a great sedative.

Some people take a 'one step at a time' approach to breaking habits. I do think that this is a positive approach, as it means realism… starting by changing one small thing instead of everything means, for many people, a greater chance of success, as it is more achievable. For me, the loss of feelings like fear, guilt and shame, and the reward of higher self-worth and self-confidence, as well as the physical benefits, brought about a domino effect of major change. Once I had stopped smoking, I became disgusted by the taste of alcohol, and couldn't be around anyone who was drinking heavily. Once I stopped drinking, I soon stopped overeating. My new thoughts about myself were of someone who was worthwhile and courageous and had won the day.

Nor did I really set a date on which change would start, although this works often well for others. As often happens, I just got sick of myself, sick of being too fat, and the slow suicide I knew would probably come with that. It wasn't about pleasing others. No one in my circle has ever been critical of my weight or thought less of me because of it. I already knew what I needed to do and why. I think most heavy people do.

I'm aware that evenings are a tricky time for me, as this is when I may be under-occupied and more likely to overeat, or binge eat, because of boredom, and of course concurrently I have more time to engage with negative thoughts which I can push down with food. I need to find something else to do at this time, and to develop the self-awareness to realise this. Again, mindfulness is a tool that enabled me to focus on my patterns of thought and behaviour, and from that challenge the things that are not working for me. I know also that if I am anxious, nine times out of ten, I am eating/drinking/smoking, and it's great to be aware of that, so I can put something in place.

That's not to say that I never enjoy a nice coffee or a meal out. They are the pleasure they have always been, an indulgence, a reward, but not an automatic negative mindless behaviour, or a palliative, or a punishment. No one really wishes it was Christmas (dinner) every day. That's the fast track to empty calories and emptier bank accounts. It's the same way here, and in the same way I am specific about what I consume, I am specific about when I can step off the gas and have a treat.

Of course, lapses in thinking and behaviour are only human. I am making a major change in my life, and as such, it needs a major change in my thinking. I'm having to come off the lie of the short-term sensation and onto the lifelong goal of feeling fit and healthy. I still dip into the cookie jar, too much, and berate myself for it, but in mindfulness, we know that every action and thought will end, and when it does, we have the gift of being aware of what happened and so learn from it.

Paradoxically, this seems to be not just about putting something in, in the form of food, alcohol or nicotine, but also letting something out – sadness, anxiety, low mood, boredom. Letting our bodies let go of stress. Letting our muscles relax. Letting our minds unlock.

Practising our new lives, one bite at a time.

8

LIVING WITH A NEED TO BE RECOGNISED AND APPRECIATED

MATT

They say the hardest thing in life is breaking up in a relationship and I would agree this is true. But a close second is to change and release old patterns of behaviour. These are so ingrained in you that unless someone points out these flaws to you, you are often powerless to see them. This is like me. I had no idea that literally everything I did was to get some kind of reaction. I would go above and beyond to help people or work overtime just to be noticed and recognised. It never occurred to me that this was my time. I was prepared to just give it up without question.

If someone needed me, I would be there. I would split myself into three and literally be there for someone in the morning, then in the afternoon and then in the evening I would be on the phone listening to someone else's worries. I had no sense of validation or self-love and would get these any way I could. Therefore, anything I did was done from a place of unknowing and just jumping headfirst without thinking. I volunteered at a charity shop just for the feel-good factor and cookies. The same was true of a playgroup; I volunteered there just to be around the children who love that you are there to play with them.

The truth is I had no idea what I needed, and my life was filled with giving 100 per cent to everyone and my work, and zero to me. I was lonelier than ever and yet never really acknowledged it, filling my time with TV series and watching video repeats of film and TV sitcoms I loved, particularly *Fresh Fields*; *French Fields*; *After Henry*; *Two Up, Two Down*; Ever Decreasing Circles; and *To the Manor Born* – all of which I found hilarious. It never occurred to me that this was avoiding life and hiding. To me, this was having fun and enjoying the nostalgia of old TV.

I was filling a missing part of me, the need to be loved, and TV and helping people gave me this in bucketloads. Still, I lived alone, suffering in silence as the price for being there for everyone. Loneliness hung onto me like a long-lost friend. I was powerless to what I was doing, being only twenty-one years old. Just thinking, 'Great, I can live in a flat on my own and have my own space'. Not realising that I was taking myself away from interacting with others unless I was at work. There, I put on my happy face and was everyone's friend. The customers at the coffee shop loved me, always looking out for me, giving me tips and writing me letters of recommendation.

To me, life seemed to be great, but it was all a lie. I was full of self-loathing and hatred for the life I had. I disappeared into anything I could to avoid feeling the pain of not being seen, validated and appreciated. I used to have my mum and brothers and sister over for dinner regularly as I loved entertaining. They would marvel at how tidy my flat was and how good the dinner was, never really checking in to see how I was. It was easy I suppose not to ask questions. We all sometimes accept what is presented to us on the surface.

This continued for years. I would go and join dance classes and never fully communicate with the people involved, just say 'Hi' and join in. I would do college courses and be too scared to let other students in, choosing instead to concentrate on the course material and on researching the topic to the degree of visiting libraries and other places rather than mixing with other students. Even supporting people over the phone for hours on end. But I was getting noticed, so what did it matter how much of my time I gave away? I knew no difference, as I had never been told I was enough or that my time was important. I joined dating sites and got nothing back in return. I was really lonely.

This only changed when I learned about Louise Hay through a friend and her mirror work. Just standing in front of the mirror and looking at yourself really is quite a feat. Crazy, I know. We look at ourselves in the mirror all the time to do our hair or look at how much acne we have or how our teeth are looking. Yet this is not really seeing

– which means looking at the person staring back at you, really staring at their eyes and then saying affirmations like, 'I love you, I really do'. Then committing to these words and really holding that feeling. To lots of people, regularly saying these words can bring tears of joy. For me, it was a smile and then a chuckle. To truly acknowledge me and the person I was.

This was the beginning of when things started to change for me. I was on the journey to no longer needing to be appreciated or recognised. This was by no means easy as every now and then I would trip myself up – spending time with friends who weren't very supportive and being in jobs that did not enable me to grow. As well as letting go of my whole personality while abroad in Portugal years later and relearning who I was and what I liked. Very revealing, I can tell you, as you never realise how much of you is not really you, but things you have taken because your parents did it.

Now I write poetry and write freely with no requirement for recognition or approval. It is my way of expressing what is going on for me. This, I realise, is more important than anything else – for me to have a voice. To be able to articulate how I am feeling and what is important to me. Poetry is the greatest ever gift to myself as I can unleash my thoughts and feelings onto paper and reveal my truths, no longer hiding and not seen.

9

TALE OF THE UNEXPECTED. THE PRIORY

SHARON

During the last year, Matt and I have discovered some wonderful heritage sites on our doorstep, and our visits there have been hugely enjoyable. We have found that on a lot of our trips, what we are noticing in ourselves and our surroundings, and our thoughts about that, really do influence how much pleasure we get from our day.

Take one of our first trips to a medieval priory, near one of the local cities.

The day hadn't started very auspiciously. It was raining, and worst of all, because of the lockdown, there was nowhere to get a coffee. No coffee! Matt and I love our coffees, so this was tantamount to a total disaster. Perhaps we shouldn't go after all?

This was my first opportunity to be mindful of my thoughts, which were running a bit like this:
- I don't do rain.
- No coffee.
- There's bound to be a lot of mud. Not pleasant. Especially on uphill slopes.
- No coffee.
- Let's call the whole thing off.

Sensibly, Matt suggested we get on the train, 'because what else are we going to do?' We did. We regrouped. I had been thinking:
1. This is bound to go wrong – we will have wasted our time and our train fare.
2. It's another thing that won't work out.
3. What is it with the Government/train company/coffee shop?
4. I really need a break. I need this day to be perfect.

Bringing mindful awareness to these thoughts meant I could start to rebalance them.
1. Thought 1 revisited: This is opinion, not fact. I can't predict with any certainty what will happen. Is there a more realistic way of looking at this?
2. Thought 2 revisited: Nothing like a bit of catastrophising. It's unrealistic and out of proportion.
3. Thought 3 revisited: I will feel more comfortable accepting things as they are. Striving to change the unchangeable will hurt.

4. Thought 4 revisited: I need to stop setting up expectations of myself, Matt and the rest of the world that are out of proportion and put pressure on all of us.

So, what happened on our 'what else are we going to do' day? We enjoyed the openness of our minds. We took a journey we had never experienced before. We didn't know the exact route to our destination when we got off the train, but we relaxed into that, avoiding the urge to fortune tell (predict what might happen without any factual evidence) or the opposite, believing that because similar situations had worked out in a certain way, this was sure to happen again. We acknowledged and accepted just what was there, knowing that we would discover something beautiful.

The priory was a wonder, with most of the exterior still intact, and set in lush countryside. The sun was shining. I commented that it was the perfect place for a mindfulness meditation. I imagined myself bathing my senses in the smell of cut grass, the sound of birdsong, the warmth of the sun and the sight of this wonderful structure, made with dedication and love, a gift to all the people there before us. Sometimes in mental health work, we ask 'How important will this event be in six months' time?' (usually as a way of putting a difficult event into proportion). My answer, in this case, would be 'vitally important' because it reminded me that a non-judgemental curiosity and a positive filter on my thoughts and emotions can bring moments of magic to life. Magic is like that last drop of fuel that we may need to get our (mental) car, or bike, or feet, over the line in harder times. It is there for all of us, and when we are able to ask, it will come.

I do believe that an 'attitude of gratitude' goes a long way towards mental health wellness. Thankfulness and pleasure in what we have can be a powerful way to lift our mood. That day, I was grateful for being able to move around when not everyone can. To be able to pay for a train journey, when not all of us have the money, and to have the space and time to enjoy my day. Some people think that having enough means having a lot financially, or having intense exposure on social media, or to have a lot of kudos by way of a job. I appreciate that mental health issues are strongly linked to poverty, and that we need enough to pay the bills. But is wealth what we need or what we think we need? Do we need to become/live like celebrities, or think we need to? Is it realistic to expect to win Strictly or MasterChef? Or are we good enough, just as we are? And if we are good enough, what does that say about how deserving we are?

My mindfulness learners have one of their biggest struggles with the concept of self-compassion. Within the groups, compassion for others is often strongly felt and, by comparison, very easy to achieve.

Equally, caring for others doesn't seem to present many problems.

It seems to me that this struggle sometimes comes from limiting beliefs starting in early life that have continued to cause stress and hurt. Some of the ones I have heard quite often are:

- Other people are more important than me/I don't count.

- I have to stay in this (bad) situation (because it's all my fault).
- I cause problems (because I am a bad/stupid/selfish person).
- I don't deserve to be happy (because of all of the above).
- I am ugly/too fat (because I am greedy with no self-control).
- I make the wrong decisions (because I am stupid).
- I am unpopular (because I am hateful).

My own belief about being less important than everyone else has been lifelong. It originated in my childhood. I knew that I was what is sometimes referred to as an 'accident'; that is, my mother's pregnancy was unplanned. It didn't feel as though this accident was a happy one. My mother seemed angry and critical a lot of the time. I knew that she was unhappy with my father.

I blamed myself. From this thought, other miseries flourished, just like the ones my service users describe. I took the blame for the families' unhappiness and resentment. I started to comfort eat and started putting on weight, which made me feel more loathsome. In adulthood, I would let people take advantage. My ex sister-in-law didn't want me with the main group at my own grandmother's funeral. I let her get away with it. My mother and brother accused me of trying to get money from my grandmother, even though she had gifted us all a sum of money, which they still had. I didn't challenge this. In later life, I became invisible. In a group, one of us would be missing. Alone, I felt at the edge of a precipice that was constantly at risk of collapsing.

The more I insisted on putting myself last, the more other people bought into it. I put up with bad relationships, disloyal friends and further abusing my body with junk food and alcohol. I tried drugs (and did inhale). I have heard it said that my own thought processes brought this self-harm about. I agree to a point. People who feel/think worthless usually don't invest much in caring for themselves. What is worth caring for? (But I still maintain that an abuser is just that, an abuser. Abuse isn't about the victim's self-esteem, family or pay grade; it's about the need for power and control in the abuser. No woman or man thinks themselves into being assaulted or raped, or being at the receiving end of domestic violence.)

I had lost touch with most of my emotions, and more particularly, the emotions of anger, sadness and grief, which I soon discovered could be pushed down with food, alcohol, dealing with other people's problems and overworking. I wasn't going to show weakness either and it would be pointless expressing any feeling of loss, because no one would listen or care. I was prescribed anti-depressant medication, but didn't take it, or only took a couple of tablets before giving up. Medication was for other, weaker people. My displacement activities and state of denial would be good enough, until it wasn't.

It took fifty years for any of this to change (and even then, it wasn't intentional – which is why I continue to feel that any positive move forward, at whatever age, is worthwhile). You may feel that the thought processes laid down in childhood are irreversible; the more realistic thought is that we all have the power to change. We are adults with the choice to think anything we like. What happens now may remind us of the past and feel painful, but it is not the same situation. Our new thoughts can become our happiness, our peace, our life.

> You have moved too carefully through your life
> Always the light within you is hooded by
> Your own protecting fingers!
> (Brian Patten)

We all have thoughts, emotions and memories that disturb us, as well as those which bring us joy and fulfilment. We also each have a choice about how to react to them, day by day, moment by moment. Our minds have many rooms and many doors; it is the ones we sit in, and the doors we open or keep closed, that make our lives.

Within our rooms are sights, sounds, tastes, aromas and belongings that we can touch. Some are welcoming and reassuring. Some bring us happiness, and sometimes some create sadness or unease. Sometimes the ones that look the most genuine are the ones that are not, and it is hard to distinguish between what we are perceiving and what is actually happening. This can lead to a focus on thoughts and feelings that are overwhelmingly negative; we come to an opinion about what is in our room/mind, when the truth is very different. We also close down any other way of seeing the situation. From this, more difficult thoughts and feelings may be created. This can be the start of signs and symptoms of depression or anxiety.

Becoming aware of our thoughts and feelings gives us the power to change our response to them; our insight is the foundation of rewriting the story, of reclaiming the narrative. We are able to observe our ever-changing thoughts and react wisely, even when they are shouting loudly and seem overwhelming.

At the same time, we have the choice to show kindness and compassion to ourselves, to take the pressure off, and to take our own helpful action. You are allowed to give yourself the space and time to make positive changes.

We would like to share our lived experience with you, and to hear yours.

May we join you?

BEING CREATIVE

What is creativity anyway? Do we all have it and if we do, why are we not all great cooks or brilliant artists. The fact is it is not that simple. Life has taught us that being creative is something that requires practice and skill and has to be learnt. From a very early age, we are taught that to be creative is something that has to be learned and practised. Do you remember the first time you cooked a meal? It probably was not a great success as you did not believe that you could really do it. The same is true of any time you have decided to do any drawing of any kind. You have not known what you are wanting to draw and believed you had to do it the way you were told to do it as a child.

So, when you start to think about it, is it really surprising that you don't feel that creative? All the facts you have about being creative are telling you that you are unable to be creative. What about creative thinking and problem-solving? Well, I can guarantee that most of you reading this book will be able to say 'Yes, I can do that'. I do sudoku and crosswords and word puzzles regularly. So, if you can problem-solve and do all these other things, then here's the thing: why do you not consider yourself creative? Well, this is a lot harder to understand and requires you to ask two important questions:

1. How important is creativity to me?
2. Why do I need to be creative?

'All the world's a stage and we are merely players'. If we are just players as Shakespeare said, then why do we need to be creative? The answer is in the word 'play' and how when we first began as babies, everything we did was through play – the understanding and learning that was undertaken to recognise the different smells, sounds and textures that we came into contact with. The problem is we have forgotten how important that was to us and have taken that early creativity for granted. We have forgotten a fundamental key that it is only through play that we are creative and can make changes in our lives.

It is through creativity that we learn and can make changes in our lives. Therefore, when we have fun, we allow ourselves to let go of our rigidity and our 'I can't do that' talk. Here are some examples:

I can't do that because:
- I don't know how to.
- My hair may get ruined.
- It's childish.
- I don't want to.
- I'm too old.
- It's stupid!
- I haven't got time.
- That's not what I do.
- I'm too busy.

How about we turn these all round to:
- I can have a go.
- I can wash my hair.
- I can have some fun.
- I will have a go.
- I want to have a go.
- It will be fun!
- I will find the time.
- I am going to do this.
- I'll make time.

You can see here that when we change all these excuses, they change to become things that you can do and want to do. Suddenly the idea of playing and being creative is not so uncomfortable and scary. It is here that you realise that you are the person who is preventing and stopping you from being creative and playing. Some ways of being creative and playing are:
- Dressing up for a fancy-dress party.

- Having a part in a local theatre group.
- Going to a murder mystery weekend.
- Making a cake.
- Decorating a room.
- Reorganising your workspace.
- Choosing different colours to highlight important papers to you.
- Doing a YouTube video.
- Eating a food you have not eaten before.
- Dancing at a party or bar.
- Taking a photo.
- Creating an album or scrapbook.
- Writing a poem or short story.

All of these things are about being creative and getting you to use a different part of your brain. When you are doing this, you are not aware of anything else, and you are focused on the activity you are involved in. This then opens you up to the acceptance of enjoyment. I say it again, enjoying life does not have to be mundane or tedious and, yes, you discover that you are allowed to enjoy yourself. You realise that in this moment nothing else matters and you let go of the worries at work, the worries in your relationship. All of this doesn't matter, and this is the key when you let go – you open yourself up to new understandings. You meet people or share your experience with other people and then they get to see you.

When you have fun, you are being you; you don't put on a work front for work and you forget about how fat, thin, small or lonely you are. This is why creativity is important because through creativity and play, you open yourself up to people seeing the real you. The person who enjoys having fun and being honest, who is prepared to get it wrong and make a mistake. The you who is being vulnerable and letting people identify and connect with you. This is when you can have a shared moment and connection with people and realise what really matters.

10

FORGOTTEN BEAUTY. THE OLD CANAL

SHARON

Our discovery of an abandoned canal, again only a short distance away but unknown to us, and I suspect many other people, was one of the jewels of our summer walks.

We had again taken a short train/bus trip, this time with coffee (yay!) The day was a blessing, very hot, with the bluest of blue sky. I was delighted to hear a skylark for the first time in decades – one of the benefits of Covid lockdown restrictions. I inwardly said 'Thank you' for this special treat. As we have said before in our book, an attitude of gratitude, including for the small things, can help to lift our mood.

Not for the first time, we had a challenge with transport! No problem with the train or the connecting bus We got off at the wrong place! We could have chosen to resent this or get annoyed with ourselves or with each other. Instead, we decided to simply go with it, and enjoy what we found, in the moment that we found it, not wanting more, or fighting to change the situation, which would probably have been stressful and eaten into the time we had to enjoy the day. My mindfulness practice has taught me to acknowledge and accept just what is there, without striving to fashion it into something else, not second-guessing the future or trying to reshape the past.

Out of the blue, we were offered a lift to the harbour (what we thought was the right one) but we decided to walk. We walked through the harbour complex, which seemed to be frequented by very wealthy people, judging by the number of private yachts and elegant facilities. Perhaps the man who offered us a lift assumed that we had a car but for some reason couldn't use it. I couldn't imagine many people using the bus, but then perhaps I was also assuming, without any facts to back up my thinking. With this particular thought, there wouldn't be a major consequence, but in terms of mental health, second-guessing situations (particularly in a negative way) can lead us into low mood and start a spiral of anxiety.

It was then that we found it.

Unlike its counterpart in the heart of the city, this stretch of canal was unkempt, the surface water covered in algae and the canal bank straggly. Yet we could also see that in returning to a more natural state, the area was teeming with beautiful wild grasses and flowers, and that birds were singing in the trees. A notice told us of the different types of birds and vegetation we could find there; like the canal, the sign was old and weathered. We could see a little further along that there were houseboats, which were decorated with plants and summer furniture, and looked occupied. It was a deeply tranquil place in which to make a home.

So, on one side of the pathway were the yachts, and feet away, the abandoned canal with its houseboats.

In my work, the word 'should' is often heard and very deep-rooted. Some of my service users are convinced they have to be perfect, for example, because someone, a long time ago, said that to be less than perfect would mean not being good enough at all, about anything. It would mean being stupid and worthless, with the humiliation and self-loathing that this feeling can bring. It means being wrong, about everything, past, present, and future. Pleasing others, not yourself (definitely not yourself). Feeling scared. Feeling inadequate, even on a yacht. Feeling not enough because we're not on a yacht.

Pressure to make ourselves and our lives more and better is all around, and for a lot of us on our mental health journey, it is exhausting and depressing, a chore that can never be completed. It takes away from bringing joy to what we have. It is pushing at a locked door to make our lives look like someone else's.

Let us allow ourselves to let our lives take the path they take, without striving and trying to fit into another individual's life. Let us bring awareness to what we need, rather than the commodities we think we want. Matt and I are unable to do this walk today because of lockdown.

When we walk this route again, we will have joy in each other's company, and awareness of the importance to both of us of our friendship. Instead of a creeping frustration and boredom born of long periods alone indoors, we will be grateful for the gift of each other's company, and the natural world so long closed off to us.

Your peace of mind is important enough to make manifest. Focusing on one thing at a time – being in nature, walking, the presence of a precious friend – brings meaning and happiness, instead of the stress caused by constantly switching tasks. We may feel that because we are tackling a lot of tasks at one time, we are making good progress, and at the same time, reducing our feelings of anxiety. But as sometimes happens, this thought is lying to us.

Rapid cycling from activity to focus and back again in quick succession means expending energy and time, and there is the risk of using one activity to avoid another one. Overall, our progress is limited.

And the 'right' harbour? I don't doubt that we will find it – and in the meantime, we will try to leave behind any feelings of anxiety about not looking, and that 'should' word, and enjoy what is alive for us, here and now, just in this moment.

11

THE REAL PICTURE

MATT

Life is often a paradox, not allowing us to see the reality of what is going on. We take on board what is transpiring without question. A chance meeting proceeds to a friendship being formed. This connection is then assumed to be something more than a chance meeting. Whilst the reality is totally different and the inability to be honest at the time leads to something other than intended.

This situation may sound strange but it is all too familiar to all of us. No matter whether it is the job you are in or the relationship. You are always presented at the inset with a truth that is attractive and appealing. This draws you in, creating a falsehood where you accept the ideas and concepts that are apparent – never thinking that things will change and become totally different to this initial appeal. Unfortunately they do and this initial truth is discarded as the gloss of a new relationship and job wears off.

Now the honeymoon period is over, so to speak, and the creaks and flaws appear. You start to feel as though things are not the way you thought they would be.

So what do you do in this situation?

Do you ignore this truth and carry on, as you are now depending on this job and wanting the relationship to work out? Or alternatively do you discuss your feelings and concerns with friends/colleagues to rationalise them? In truth, how you respond is up to you so long as you recognise your truth.

When you follow your truth, then you are not denying your feelings. Don't get me wrong, this is not an overnight occurrence and can take years. Sharon and I have been working on this most of our lives and are still learning. The most important thing is to recognise what your needs are. Not the needs of the company you work for or the relationship you are in. No, your personal needs. By this, I mean: what in your life makes you sing, literally? What is it that really makes your heart beat faster? What makes you feel a sense of 'Wow!'?

This is the real picture, the essence of you and why we are ending with this chapter. The rest is now down to you, literally. You have read about our experiences and journey. Now it is your turn to discover what is special and meaningful to you.

There will be something and you will know exactly what it is. Everyone has something and often need the time and space to remember what it is. Mine is writing and

I'm so glad to have found it again after years of absence. I feel truly alive and connected when I'm writing. Sharon's is her mindfulness and teaching others to just stop and experience life and its beauty. What's yours?

As Susan Jeffers says:
'Dare to connect with life.'

BIBLIOGRAPHY

Black, R M (2011), *The Definitive Book of Body Language*, Orion House, London

Kubler Ross, E (1969), *On Death and Dying*, Macmillan, New York